WILLIAM'S ANATOMY
poetry for medical students

ERIK VAN ACHTER

WILLIAM'S ANATOMY
copyright (c) 2024
All rights reserved.

No part of this book may be used
or reproduced in any manner
without written permission
except in the case of reprints
in the context of reviews.

ISBN | 9789464513028
www.erik.vanachter.com

Cover Art | Gabriel Green (U.K.)
Typesetting and Design | Kexastudio Publishing

Play back for me in memory
the photos of my ancient past
as I dance with the dreams,
knowing that all that seems to be
begins and ends with the senses.

All reality, honour-bound to appear
within the flickering spaces
behind and between the eyes,
to star in this wonderful movie
that I only know as vision.

Excerpt from
Streaming p.82-83

Foreword

I am delighted to be a small piece in this unique friendship
with a professor turned student.
A connection forged from across the world:
poetry and medicine combined to show off the art of anatomy -

I once asked Erik what he knew about medicine before he started.
I asked William Allison:

*"What did Erik know about medicine
before he started these tutorials?"*

Their answer was quite similar:
both smiled, didn't say anything and stared at me.
So I knew the answer: as good as nothing.

Four years later, I one day received the top results of nineteen
medical courses of such top-class universities as Harvard,
Yale, Johns Hopkins and Imperial College (London),
to name only a few.

From my perspective, now a jr doctor, this is almost
unbelievable and I suspect both teacher and student must have
learnt a lot and must have enjoyed the experience
very much.

And as they recently decided to continue,
I think that they will continue forever -
I may probably suggest that a new book of poetry
will arise as a sequel to this volume too?

I'm excited to see what the next chapter will entail -
Maybe a Dictionary of Anatomy?

WILLIAM MARSH, MD
Winchester UK

Table of CONTENTS

WHISPERS OF THE INNER COSMOS	9
MECHANICS OF THE FLESH	29
THE TEMPEST WITHIN	51
ECHOES OF THE MORTAL VESSEL	75
SERENADE OF THE SOMATIC SENSES	93

WHISPERS OF THE INNER COSMOS

ERIK VAN ACHTER

Searching the Heart for You

Where does my love for you sleep?
Is it divided between the ventricles,
great chambers of the left and right,
or resting in the gardens of an atrium?

I have stood at every valve searching.
Tricuspid, mitral, pulmonary,
at no valve do you flow through
and yet I know you in my blood.

Did you hide in one of the arteries,
unable to handle being watched?
Are you in the crowded aorta,
surfing silently upon my red cells?

WILLIAM'S ANATOMY

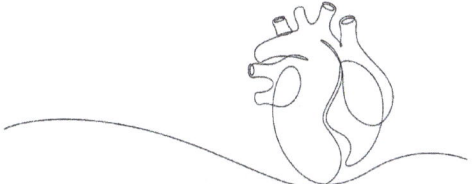

I know not even the colour of our love.
A vivid red? A frigid blue?
If I only knew how well it breathes.
May it never be choked for air.

Though I doubt it ever could.
You are, after all, *my oxygen.*
If I cannot find you swimming here,
perhaps it is only

        because you are everywhere.

ERIK VAN ACHTER

INVOCATION OF THE MUSES

Sing the complexities of art and science
deep into my frontal lobe,
sandboxed by sulcus on either side
and let me dream, sweetly
of what it means to be human.
Let the complex plans of day to day
drill their mark deep into me,
for I shall comprehend.

Let it all flow through the parietal.
Process my senses,
each and every one,
as if you were filing experiences
into a great old computer.
Press two pens onto my arm
and I shall count them with my skin.
My complexity shall forever win.

WILLIAM'S ANATOMY

Cradle the hippocampus,
so many memories that define me,
into the soft cushioned sea
of the temporal. Tempt me
with temporary flashes
of insight behind my eyes, my ears.
Shock me awake with small lightning,
with realizations in the moment.

And of all things, allow me to see.
Make me occipital. Make me unclouded.
Give unto me the many visions
straight from the divine bosom
of the eye. Let all of the world
slosh up my nerves and upward.
Bring me to life, complete,
and let this newborn brain define me.

ERIK VAN ACHTER

Controlling Now...

Connect me to myself, Brainstem.
  Let the neurons in my far reaches
    tickle each other gently,
      teasing out data with every touch,
        from my fingertips to my nether regions,
          all for the sake of sharing it back,
            back all the way to the noble beginnings
          of you, throne of the nervous systems.

          Regulate me. Hire Medulla Oblongata
         to be the general manager of my chest.
          Pay her in stimulations and chemicals
            as she does her best to keep me moving,
          pumping, breathing, visibly alive.

WILLIAM'S ANATOMY

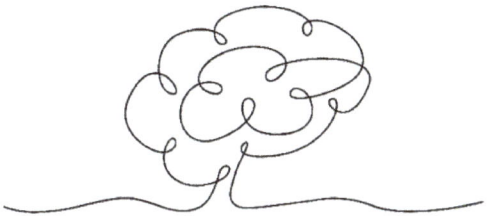

Let Secretary Pons run your hallways
  for he has so much work to do.
    Cerebellum and Thalamus rely on little Pons.
     May he and Medulla always get along,
      however hard her days may be.

        Hype me up, Midbrain, devilish middle manager,
         forever petty for not being promoted to the brain,
        taking up even its name in defiance,
         even as you grit your teeth and read the memos.
        Your offices are tight and narrow, I know.
        Hang in there, Brainstem, hang in there.

ERIK VAN ACHTER

Automated Needs System

Autonomic, robotic, self-assigned,
Nervous in name, bold in design,
Systematic, automatic, simplified.

Colour me sympathetic, guilty of feeling,
leashed by a fight-or-flight response,
ready to flee at a moment's notice,
ready to fight when the time is right.

Dragged about by a hypothalamus,
collared to my spine, the chain that binds me,
entwined in a network of nerve fibers,
alive by default, organs pumping, squirming,
like so many worms buried inside me,
latched together by the whims of the flesh.

Or parasympathetic. Buried in needs.
Feed and breed. Rest and digest.
Dampen the feeling, embrace the feeling.
Either way life happens each day.

WILLIAM'S ANATOMY

I sneeze, I cough, I vomit, I live.
My body chooses arousal or fear.
I know not control for I only live here.

Sometimes enteric, or perhaps only seeming.
I feel a desire and then I become it.
Pluck at my inherited puppet strings.
Let my brainstem have all of my things.

Control me, patrol me, swing me around.
I'll be a scent. I'll be a sound.
Squeeze reactions out of me.
Set my human instincts free.

I am an animal, meant to be
obsessed, possessed by ancient needs.
Eat it. Touch it. Do it. Live it.
Pump my vessel full of blood.
Inner and outer, working in tandem.
I am controlled. Or am I random?

ERIK VAN ACHTER

The Lines are Drawn

Narrow tubes of muscles
through which the red and blue traffic
finds so many avenues
yet never reaches an ending
for it cycles and it circles
and it reaches every crack
yet it always finds a path
that will surely lead it back.

>   You may not bring your red
>   into the counties of the blue
>   for the borders are important,
>   evidence of the goods processed,
>   the trades made, the produce presented,
>   yet there is no resentment.

WILLIAM'S ANATOMY

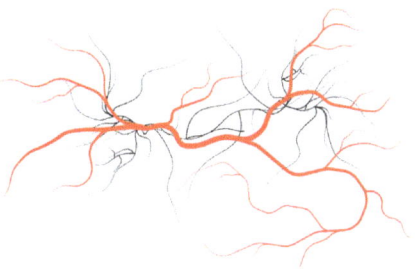

The veins versus the arteries.
The blues versus the reds.
Yet if either did become the other
then surely you'd be dead.

        Ask not for the maps to be redrawn
        for they were made with care.
        The separation between them
        is as crucial as the air.

ERIK VAN ACHTER

In and Out

Air is sensed two different ways
  and travels different paths.
    The air of a green and open field
     is different from that of a bath.

        Whiffed or swallowed, down it goes,
        forced ever further inside.
        And when it reaches an eager lung
        it finds a warm place to hide.

            The refreshing scent of oxygen.
             The taste of salt floating from the sea.
            So much of all that we perceive
             comes from the air we breathe.

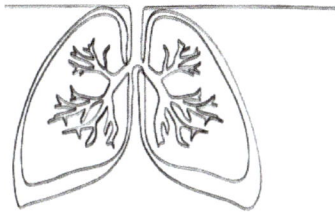

Come home, come home, into me
 where I might break you down.
  I am conversion, down to the cell.
   I am your new and humble town.

   Travel my rivers of crimson red
    and listen to the pulse of the living.
     I grant you a glimpse of creation
      in exchange for all you are giving.

ERIK VAN ACHTER

Immune

I fear we cannot hide much longer,
for we are now fugitives in this flesh,
hunted relentlessly by its police.

A neutrophil passes by on patrol,
its red and blue sirens wailing,
pale of face and eyes piercing.

I hold you in my arms, cursing.
Why did we run away here?
Far away, we hear it approach.

The growling stomach of a macrophage.
You chuckle, no longer afraid,
your eyes hollow and empty.

WILLIAM'S ANATOMY

Even in the face of death you muse,
amused that those lowly monocytes
did grow to be our greatest enemy.

We should have killed them then.
But the militant T-cells marched nearby,
their barracks loaded up.

I look out at it all. Such tranquility.
Rivers of red blood. Islands of fat.
How could we have ever known?

The antibodies have spotted us.
Now, like you, *I laugh.*
What made us think we would win?

ERIK VAN ACHTER

Failing Follicles

So much pride depends upon
the follicles, foisting a choice,
a question on men eventually:
Is baby-bald beautiful to you?

Do you laugh at the shafts
of hair that do not care for you
in old age, or turn the page?

Whether the root sheath, inner or outer,
contains anything at all, do you fall
to your knees and beg at what's left?

Nay. Do not. Even if the bulb rots
and nothing grows, no medulla,
no cortex or cuticle, and you live hairless,
be fair to that failing follicle, for it tried.

It is not a red wheelbarrow
upon which to bury your burdens.
If it did do anything at all,
it would only do so by a hair.

ERIK VAN ACHTER

De Humani Corporis Fabrica

Our identities are etched across books of flesh
fitted to these frail and mortal forms,
from race to gender to age, all penned out,
whether we accept those words or not.
Yet we tear at it, we scratch at it,
we rip away as much as we can, greedily,
leaving behind such gross and empty patches
that we then fill with law, reason, artificial things.

Take then the man who did nothing, often.
How beautiful and broad he was,
how comfortable wearing his own skin,
his own story as if he knew it to be a gift.
How vapid his expressions, how empty his head,
to just wander aimlessly past shelves,
wanting for nothing and taking nothing.
Imagine, then, how envious I was of that.

WILLIAM'S ANATOMY

Do not blame me, I beg of you,
I, who am so uncomfortable within my book
of flesh to which I have been prescribed
for my envy, my desire, my lust for his life
if I had to carve him up, quietly, gently,
artfully sliding a Stanley knife
between the teres major and latissimus dorsi,
creating new leather, and a brand-new cover.

MECHANICS OF THE FLESH

ERIK VAN ACHTER

The Mysterious Mister Spleen

Not a single student who studies here
knows where Mister Spleen
first got his enigmatic nickname.

Surely he is and always has been
the soul of the school, or so we believed.
It seemed impossible to conceive
of a world in which he walks away,
leaving a generation of scholars
to never know his name.

We never knew why
he stockpiled red things, so much red
until the day we needed them most.
Then, like a hurricane, he handed them out
and suddenly all the halls were merry.

WILLIAM'S ANATOMY

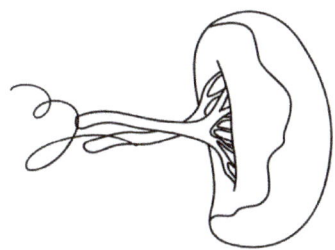

Some say he rules his class with an iron fist
yet he never seemed to stand out to me.
Perhaps a rumor since he trains prefects
to roam the halls, always watching,
always ready to act on his command.

Yet he only ever waves his hand
and smiles, serenely, as if dreaming.
We thought he was the soul of the school
until he retired, his eyes still gleaming.

ERIK VAN ACHTER

DOCTOR B

Doctor B winds up his plasma blaster,
prepared to launch once more,
as a fading memory glimmers into view.
This problem is not new
for he has seen it before, this veteran.

Already, he had the countermeasure.
A premium antidote made by hand,
developed in the lab carefully
so as to prevent the great horrors
that happened the last time.

WILLIAM'S ANATOMY

They will not happen this time.
He taps on the old bones, gently,
his birthplace at the back of his mind,
as he soars off toward the invaders,
his blaster gleaming and loaded.

Nothing shall tear down this home,
these narrow red streets,
nor shall a single enemy escape.
Let all who have tried before
fear the avenging chemist.

ERIK VAN ACHTER

The Traffic Cop

Faithful Epiglottis works hard, as always.
His curvy smile pervades the streets
as he blows his whistle,
guiding traffic this way and that.

> So close to the factories
> where oxygen tanks are made,
> letting them through for hours a day.

Yet sometimes, twice or thrice a day,
the food trucks pass by
on their way to festivals elsewhere
that he is never invited to.

> He sighs, and with a wave of his hand
> all the airflow stops, for a moment,
> so that food may go where it must.

WILLIAM'S ANATOMY

He knows not where the burgers and fries
and tacos and funnel cakes go
nor is it his job to find out.

       Yet he does wonder, twice or thrice a day,
       why they share such an important road.
       Would it not make more sense, he muses,
       to give the oxygen a road of his own?

Still, it is not his job to think.
His job is quiet and easy and necessary
and that is enough for Epiglottis.

ERIK VAN ACHTER

Joining of the Families

We gather here, beneath these bronchi trees,
to bear witness to the holy union
between the great old families
of Circulatory and Respiratory.

May the marriage of Capillary and Vein
last forevermore, breathing new life
into these ancient and storied legacies.
May this bond pump fresh blood
into these two famous houses.

Let this moment wash over the cells
in the great body of the Lord
so that he might bless this day.

WILLIAM'S ANATOMY

If anyone has any objection,
any reason as to why these two
should not be wed, speak now.
Or forever hold your breath.

By the power vested in me,
I now pronounce you husband and wife,
until death do you part.
Share your every breath.
May your hearts beat as one.

You may now kiss the bride.

ERIK VAN ACHTER

The Exchange

Here we barter, our canisters never leaking,
for the gases inside are far too precious.
How much oxygen will you give
for my carbon dioxide if I beg?

Your uniform is so much cleaner than mine,
yet we both wear the same deep red.
We both bring inner tubes with us,
always ready to swim at a moment's notice.

And our work is hard, of course.
Yours surely no easier than mine,
though you have more experience.
Still, my products are made in a lab.

So many hours and days in a coat
spent turning one gas into another
only to have something you call waste
just so that I can trade with you.

WILLIAM'S ANATOMY

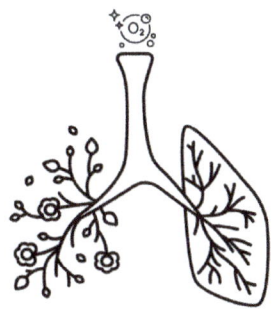

Your oxygen was found outside,
plucked from the air as if picking apples,
so readily accessible, so easy,
yet you have the nerve to judge me?

Sure, my uniform is a bit smudged.
Would yours not be if we traded places?
Alas, we can't. You have your route
and I have mine. This we cannot trade.

Only the gases, yours more noble than mine,
can ever be exchanged, however I barter.
How unfair and unfitting, I think,
but it is not for me to say it.

ERIK VAN ACHTER

LAMENTATIONS OF THE ALVEOLUS STAFF

We heard the red cells complaining again.
The hours are long and hard.
The exchange rates unforgiving.
Security is brutal and occasionally makes mistakes
but what did they expect here?

Being hired to Alveolus is an honour.
Do they not know this?
Do they not look upon our great factories,
the towering, rounded bulbs,
the impressive motions of the diaphragm
as it shifts the very ground beneath us,
and marvel in what we have built?

But no, they don't, for they are whining.
Of bumping into cholesterol on the roads.
Of their sugar levels being a little off.

WILLIAM'S ANATOMY

Yes, yes, we know your job is hard
but we can't control everything, you know?
We send your complaints, every last one,
up to Central, or at least we try to,
but that's all we can do.

So much is out of our hands,
here in middle management,
but the red cells don't know or care.
They just moan and groan, day in, day out,
all because of so many things
that we here cannot control.

ERIK VAN ACHTER

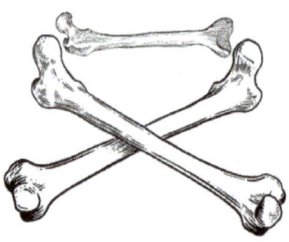

Dice on the Tarsal Peninsula

Carve some dice with friend Talus
and throw them twice into the chasm,
hoping to roll snake eyes again.

But do not be surprised if Calcaneus,
being the cheating heel that he is,
plays with loaded dice to win.

So long as Navicular is away at sea,
piloting boats to who knows where,
letting any bet stand will be a gamble.

WILLIAM'S ANATOMY

Roll your cuboid little dice anyway,
content that maybe you'll win today,
but do not complain if you are nagged.

A middle-aged woman in wedges watches,
wife of Talus, her eyes ever annoyed.
She surely curses him in ancient cuneiform.

Her sister is often intermediate,
blocking her elder's blows,
since Talus often makes her violent.

Lateral to both of them sits their friend,
her eyes quietly pointed away,
unwilling to watch this idiocy.

Oh Navicular, Navicular, come home.
Back to the Tarsal Peninsula
so that you might keep the peace,
fresh from your foolish travels.

ERIK VAN ACHTER

Beware the Leukocytes

The leukocytes are hunting tonight.
Best be on guard and do nothing suspicious,
for should you draw their attention,
you shall be a bitter lunch for them to swallow.

They care not for the sharpened knives
of the T-Cells nor the chemistry of the B-Cells.
Chemical warfare? Pre-made weapons?

No, give a leukocyte only its own fangs
and watch it bite fiercely into everything.
In packs, alone, it does not matter.
All that arouses suspicion is food.

WILLIAM'S ANATOMY

Yet how blind, how senseless, how broad
their violence can sometimes be.
Are the charges they are meant to protect
inflamed, injured, bleeding, broken?

A leukocyte will not slow or stop
for it is not healing that drives them.
Only an endless hunger is felt.

When gluttony is your only emotion
and feeding your only cause
it can be hard to see, at times,
how beneficial a beast could be.

ERIK VAN ACHTER

Twin Towns

Trachea. How strange to think
that this narrow route
with so very much traffic
has always and ever been
right next to my hometown
of Esophagus.

    Yet look how pristine
    her travelers look.
    So light and airy
    as they glide on by,
    floating quietly, quickly
    down well-kept streets.

        All while the slimy roads
        of my neighbourhood
        allow anything to pass.

WILLIAM'S ANATOMY

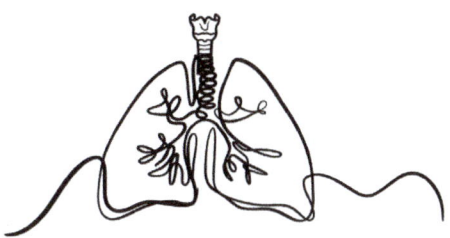

Cheese and grease and salt
line the gutters here.
So much is gross
and fat and smelly.

    Is this the difference
    between a highway and a byway?
    The cleanliness, the class?
    I would gladly, in a heartbeat,
    move my home to Trachea,
    if only I were ever asked.

ERIK VAN ACHTER

March of the Platelet

Strange and nimble thrombocytes,
ever eager to hug and to hold,
like a thick ivy that responds to open air.

Let fly the colours of coagulation,
the rhythmic drumbeat of a thousand platelets
marching off to heal the wounded,
their banners soft like clouds.

A senseless hoard with no nucleus
yet organised to a singular purpose
only scarcely remembering
a vague past life as bone marrow.

WILLIAM'S ANATOMY

Perhaps it is this history that drives them.
Born so deep within the white of bone,
perhaps the open skies beyond the flesh
draws them out naturally, as if dreaming
of being as far from the inside as possible.

Yet these little ones, too, must stay.
And so they clump together,
shoulder to shoulder, trying with vigor
to at least glimpse the outside.

How funny that their desire to be free
might have made them elites,
a critical cell of warrior brothers
who stave off all misfortune proudly.

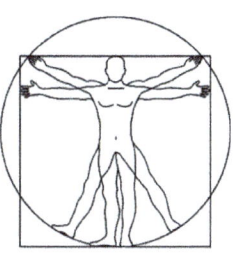

THE TEMPEST WITHIN

Awakening

Deep in the swollen glands of the mansion,
the black blood of a bile-filled heart was beating,
its vile vibrations assailing the stale air,
strictly stagnant, yet alive with spite.

Far off in the upper floors, beneath the attic
old half-rotten fluids pumped
for the first time since the collapse
of the lineage, and the dripping of chemicals
from a great iron thyroid began.

Dim lights came on in glassy-eyed windows
as spider webs floated like veins,
vast expanses of dusty air trapped in them.

WILLIAM'S ANATOMY

Room temperatures started to stabilise.
The soggy red carpet of the front door
licked at the dry, cracked doorframe.

It was thirsty. Pipes that hadn't run in years
suddenly flooded with thick old liquid.
Tree branches ran their fragile fingers
over the blemished skin of the outer walls.

A sour grin seemed to cover the moon.
So much to do after a long sleep.
So many needs to satisfy right away.

ERIK VAN ACHTER

Orchards of air

The trunk of the rare Air-Fruit tree
splits into so many branches
on both the left and the right sides.
Soft leaves form it up into lobes,
as branches break smaller and smaller.

Ah but the fruits, the titular fruits.
Covered in miniscule veins
where cells of the tree
meet the itty-bitty seeds.
What a wondrous time
to trade oxygen for carbon dioxide.

WILLIAM'S ANATOMY

A thin membrane masks it all,
  forming up walls, soft and slick,
    that protect the whole of the tree.

      How tricky, then, to harvest the fruit.
        To take a bite of fresh air
          from the boughs of the wood.

            Thank goodness for Old Man Diaphragm,
              for if anyone can regulate this orchard,
              it must surely be him,
                  his bald dome bobbing down the rows.

ERIK VAN ACHTER

Left's Failure

Left kidney turned to right
and asked her promptly:
What are you doing tonight?

Left turned away, blushing red.
I wouldn't know, silly.
Why don't you ask the head?

Left tried to send a signal out
but soon after started to pout.
Brain didn't care to answer his call.
Left wondered if he cared at all.

WILLIAM'S ANATOMY

His ureter pulsed as he thought.
What other options has he got?
Well if I don't listen, he realised,
Brain will have to hear my cries.

Left stopped filtering right then.
He ignored his job, begged for attention.
Right sobbed, handling both sections.

Brain noticed but did not say a word.
Left would regret that he'd been heard.
In no time at all, Brain shut Left down,
without a mention, with only a frown.

One transplant later and Left was free
but not in the way he'd hoped to be.

ERIK VAN ACHTER

In Utero

Frivolous fallopian tubes
formed up from the fundus
at the top of this tiny world.
Inside it all, a baby girl.

The seed of life given form,
torn from unknown nothingness,
reaching, kicking, to no one in particular.

Cervix, cervix, hold strong.
The vigor of a fetus challenges you,
but let the umbilical cord do
what it sets out to,
gradually, gently, calming cravings.

Mid-gestation, everything holds.
Stretched, pulled, bludgeoned, bent.
Yet these walls keep, well as ever.
Cleverly designed for a life's needs.

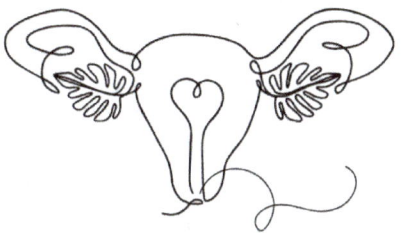

The greed of the babe knows no bounds
and so many nutrients nourish it.
A small price to pay for the gift of creation.

Stem cells evolve into shapes evolve into organs.
Something special takes shape.
And for a brief period of time
two worlds collide inside one body.

ERIK VAN ACHTER

Sternum's Cubs

Sternum shot a glance inward.
Her cubs were still safe inside.
The members of her pack
encircled the vital area,
borrowing strength from her
through the Costal Cartilage,
their connections firm and flexible.

The floaters hung at the rear of the pack.
Amidst both true and false loyalists,
they alone denied the Cartilage Pact.

The riblike walls of the den
would keep out the rain, certainly,
but dangers traveling along tunnels,
through the vertebrae of the woods
would still be deadly, fierce.

WILLIAM'S ANATOMY

One of the floating packmates barked.
A rumour started, idle gossip, banter.
But it destabilised the ranks.

A single rib of the den cracked.
Sternum ran over to the cubs, quickly,
her broad body absorbing the blow,
taking a deft, decisive stance.

All devotees of the Costal Cartilage sprinted.
Some were loyal. Some were not.
But none could afford Sternum's death.
They lifted and they laboured.
And in thirty gruelling minutes of digging,
Sternum was set free, slightly bent but alive.
And not a single cub beneath her was harmed.

ERIK VAN ACHTER

White and Yellow Ships

Once again, the ports were all full.
The old captain sighed, weary.
The bureaucrats of the Prostate
held all the cards, firm in hand.

He hated how they bounced about
before deciding which ships to sail.
Seamen of the navy stood ready to go
but a fleet of trash ships blocked them.

Who to go? Who to go?
He already knew the flow.
The trash, of course, had to go.

WILLIAM'S ANATOMY

The seamen's quest was vital, sure,
but it was just a hunting expedition.
While every good empire needs eggs,
streets full of trash do not function.

The large yellow barges
blew loud their horns
and sailed out into the open sea.

Far behind, the pristine white naval ships
could only curse and shout and whine.
Their hunting trip would have to wait
for a more convenient time, tomorrow.

ERIK VAN ACHTER

An Ode to the Overworked Pancreas

Pancreatic, just like magic,
systematic, rarely tragic,
one part digestive, exocrine,
one part hormonal, endocrine.

    Regulate my sugar, baby,
    pace me proper, maybe save me.
    Bicarbonate me with a boom.
    Neutralise the acidic doom
    while well-timed enzymes all consume
    my carbs and fats if I have room.

        Get me running extra well
        with your sweet internal touch.
        I don't ask for much
        but I'll make you work.
        And maybe you'll think
        that I'm a jerk,
        but don't shirk your duties.

WILLIAM'S ANATOMY

I promise, babe, no alcohol.
I know you can't take it all,
so make me function proper, doll,
while I eat cake and take a call.

        Sweeten the deal with insulin.
        We can't let diabetes win.
        Keep me healthy, despite my greed.
        Pancreas, you're what I need.

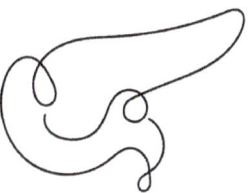

ERIK VAN ACHTER

A Cord

A thin cable runs from seat to skull,
a cord entrapped in a nerve,
ready to serve, except in a pinch,
ironic though that may be.

A bulbous pulpous nucleus,
fat and full of so much significance,
wearing bones as corsets,
as if trying to slim down.

Processes behind and beside.
Miniscule spikes, as of a dinosaur,
but there is no roar in here.
Only the gentle bending of a pillar.

WILLIAM'S ANATOMY

How strangely thin this tower.
So much more compact
than a skyscraper, an antenna,
or even most motherboards.

What an efficient computer,
oddly shaped though it is
and bordering on peripheral
when compared to the mainframe.

Yet it does so very well
as it spells out each sensation,
creating feelings where none were.
How wonderful to know it works.

ERIK VAN ACHTER

A Fireball

If "S" stands for super, then our collars are nice,
where the letter is spelled out sideways, twice.
Two clavicles, twin sisters,
serving the sternum,
or perhaps the shoulder blades.

Ah, but the blades. How poetic, how prophetic
that the slender curve of a clavicle,
the beautiful bends and flow
would go seamlessly into a broad blade,
hidden behind the back, as if to say:
Come at me. I am human.

To have two, yes two, of these blades.
To threaten to whip two separate arms
rapidly into position,
orbs and hinges creaking
as our weak little limbs
flap into place, deceptively strong,
though not as long as the legs.

WILLIAM'S ANATOMY

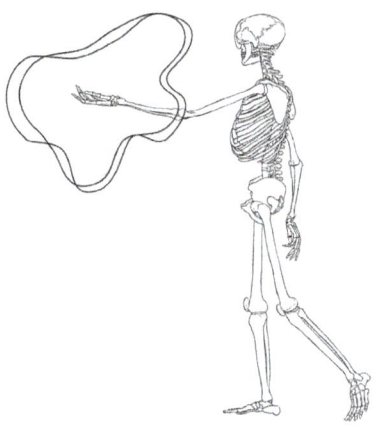

So much length, contained in a femur,
so much strength, contained in a kick,
powered by a few petty neurons,
safely tucked away in the brainbox,
commanding the body:
We do not flee. Fight.

Yes, yes, hormones enrage me.
Cage me in a feeling of animalistic impulse,
so that I might know I am still here,
still a fireball contained in a fleshy purse.

ERIK VAN ACHTER

Requesting Lobes

Sing the complexities of art and science
deep into my frontal lobe,
sandboxed by sulcus on either side
and let me dream, sweetly
of what it means to be human.
Let the complex plans of day to day
drill their mark deep into me,
for I shall comprehend.

Let it all flow through the parietal.
Process my senses,
each and every one,
as if you were filing experiences
into a great old computer.
Press two pens onto my arm
and I shall count them with my skin.
My complexity shall forever win.

WILLIAM'S ANATOMY

Cradle the hippocampus,
so many memories that define me,
into the soft cushioned sea
of the temporal. Tempt me
with temporary flashes
of insight behind my eyes, my ears.
Shock me awake with small lightning,
with realizations in the moment.

And of all things,
allow me to see.
Make me occipital. Make me unclouded.
Give unto me the many visions
straight from the divine bosom
of the eye. Let all of the world
slosh up my nerves and upward.
Bring me to life, complete,
and let this newborn brain define me.

ERIK VAN ACHTER

Victim of the Sinuses

Beneath the brow, the sinuses.
Let them behave, let them behave,
though they so often may not.

Push not against the nasal bone,
tender, ticklish sinus.
My cartilage, my cushions
are so much further down,
above my frown, below my crown.

WILLIAM'S ANATOMY

Vex me not, noble sinus.
Respect the septum's borders.
For I would gladly have order,
please, if you would allow it.

Frontal sinus, frontal sinus.
You, especially, are on thin ice.
You never did play nice
and did you think that I,
while wisdom teeth were growing,
would live on, never knowing
of your unfortunate sensitivities?

Your proclivities tire me, sinus.
Let me breathe, let me rest.
I have already done my best.

ECHOES OF THE MORTAL VESSEL

ERIK VAN ACHTER

Across the Pink Sea

Oh papillae, oh papillae,
many bumps upon the Pink Sea,
how much you mean to me.

      Let your small sandbars
      tickle the base of my raft
      yet I shall not crash, oh bumps,
      for I trust in the great median.

           Down Lingual Sulcum I sail.
           This river, beset on either side
           by your filliforms and fungiforms
           shall ever be my faithful guide.

WILLIAM'S ANATOMY

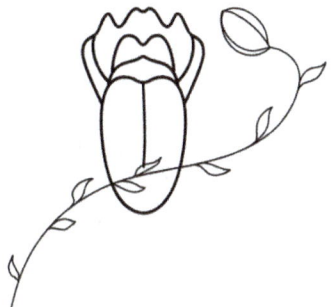

Your waves buckle and undulate,
as if to taste at my spoon-like oars.
Ha! Try your best to sink me, then.

        I see clearly the terminalis,
        noble rear of the Pink Sea's maw.
        And though I know much remains,
        I fear no sea monsters nor whorls,
        for you all mean naught to me.

ERIK VAN ACHTER

Me and My Ginglymus

Many a ginglymus merges in me
and I move and I lock and I pop
as my hinges all move into place
or flap about in 3D space.

Shift my position, my many joints,
for I rest easy on my cartilage.
I am balls and sockets and hinges,
clicking about where they will.

WILLIAM'S ANATOMY

    I kick the ball. I run ahead.
        Go, go, gleeful ginglymus!
            The simple joints. The compound joints.
              Synovial, gliding, mechanical.

                I am your machine. You are my gears.
                  Grind me onward, backward, upward.
                  Lock into place like plastic pieces
                    and I shall always be your toy.

ERIK VAN ACHTER

Maw of the World

We who feed upon collagen and calcium
shall now begin this meeting.
Speak now, members of the council
or forever hold your peace.

We, the incisors, stand with the canines.
Let there be cutting, ripping, and tearing.
May all foods imprisoned within
be beholden to our authority,
for it is we who guard the border.

We, the cuspids, may be few in number
but we are strong and relentless.
We have earned our nickname,
for we will hunt like hounds.
Allow us the honour of critical points,
for our grip shall be merciless
and our blades ever ready to act.

WILLIAM'S ANATOMY

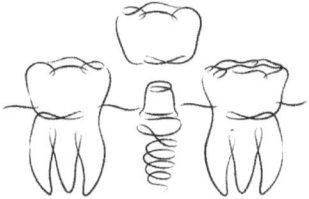

We, the premolars, shall be the yellow tape.
None who enter here may pass
until they are crushed and ground down
into an even more reasonable size.
Let all who pass us shrink.

Forget not the many, we molars.
With our wisdom and our might combined,
allow no stray food to go unpunished.

United we stand, then, we of the council.
May all who pass our whitened borders
fear the surnames of the noble Teeth.

Streaming

Cranial nerve two, circuit of vision,
emissary of the optical vesicle,
vehicle for all I might ever see,
let your cables snap and crackle
so that I might instantly peruse
the contents of a room, a face.

Show me that space, the majesty
of visual data, the great illusions.
Tickle the middle cranial fossa,
dot the x of the great chiasm
betwixt the eyes and spark up.

Shoot your lightning thoughts
throughout the mind, instantly,
so that all my other senses
might tremble before the king.

WILLIAM'S ANATOMY

Retinas glistening and gleaming,
while the blind spots are dreaming,
all rods and cones screaming,
beneath the weight of sight,
the infinite speed of a photograph
snapped, recorded, added quick
to the endless, growing stream.

Play back for me in memory
the photos of my ancient past
as I dance with the dreams,
knowing that all that seems to be
begins and ends with the senses.

All reality, honour-bound to appear
within the flickering spaces
behind and between the eyes,
to star in this wonderful movie
that I only know as vision.

ERIK VAN ACHTER

Sounds from the Bone

Some may snicker like fools
at the floating hyoid bone,
detached, ostracised from the skeleton,
uninvited to their weddings
as it flaps about, seemingly alone.

They know not, I daresay,
that it eloped with the larynx,
so entranced it was
by the harp-strings of the voice box,
so eager to be a part of a chorus.

WILLIAM'S ANATOMY

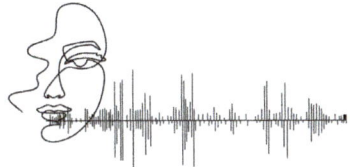

And now a duet, a lovely pairing,
a gentle caring clapping of the parts.
How many sounds might remain voiceless
were it not for the hyoid's support
in the shadows of the throat?

Let not the lavish balls
thrown in the court of the ribcage
distract you from this estranged nobleman,
he who happily married an artist,
and lived eternally in bliss.

ERIK VAN ACHTER

The lady on the Turkish saddle

Oh great Sella Turcica, saddle of the head,
seat upon which so much rests,
you tiny little forgettable piece
of the most significant bones.

Does Sir Pituitary love you?
Or does he spit upon you
from you, his tiny throne,
and the hypophyseal fossa,
thinking himself greater and grander
because he, at least,
comes up in conversation.

WILLIAM'S ANATOMY

Rejoice milady Sella, tiny Turkish bit
of the many-splendoured skull.
You are small, you are barely grown,
yet you are known, to some.

May your marriage hold water
for surely Sir Pituitary must love you,
cradling you between the locked doors
of the chiasmatic groove, hidden away.
You live in so much secrecy
but you are still a celebrity
in your own tiny, bony way.

ERIK VAN ACHTER

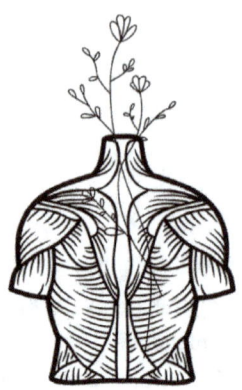

Disorder on the Back Row

The siblings Teres sang from the back,
in both major and minor keys,
rivaled by the nearby Rhomboids,
so very short and tightly huddled.

Their notes complimented one another
yet both sets of brothers fought with volume
for the attentions of fair Lumbar Fascia.
Trapezius only sighed, craning his neck.

WILLIAM'S ANATOMY

Fair Fascia would not commit to them,
only retreating further into her seat,
becoming nearly concave as she hid,
twisting and turning away from gazes.

Latissimus Dorsi chuckled at her shyness.
He was broad, central to the back row.
If the antics of the back were not scolded,
it was only because of the example he set.

Rectus Abdominus squirmed in his seat.
Surely this mischief would break the song.
He wondered, watching back and front,
how long until the conductor grew sore.

ERIK VAN ACHTER

STATE VS. APPENDIX: JUDGE BRAIN PRESIDING

Count Vermiform Appendix, resident of the core.
You stand accused of the crime
of Appendicitis, which we do not take lightly.

It is alleged that your charitable housing
for our allies, the beneficial bacteria,
the flora and fauna of the gut
was all a cover for your recent atrocities.

We did not judge you for your worm shape,
nor for stapling yourself to Cecum
in his abode betwixt the small and the large.

WILLIAM'S ANATOMY

We surely did not begrudge you that,
nor did we besmirch your name
for it was well-known, publicised even,
that our mucosal immune functions
owe much to your charitable donations.

Yet now, you have chosen to inflame.
We know not if you have noble reasons.
Perhaps you have swollen your estate
only in some strange act of self-defence?

Regardless, the evidence has stuck.
Though we thank you for your service,
you are hereby sentenced to Appendectomy.
May your bloated body rest in peace.

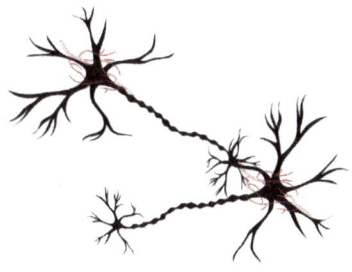

SERENADE OF THE SOMATIC SENSES

ERIK VAN ACHTER

Behind The Clouds

Gather up the traffic cones
and all the rods you can.
Flash the streetlight's colour.

Truly, it was a foggy day.
Old gray clouds fight our efforts
yet we try and we try.

Keep that round window clear.
Paint a vivid coloured ring around
so that all know who lives here.

WILLIAM'S ANATOMY

Our city's vast and vitreous body
shall not yield to darkness yet.
Quickly, clean the great dome!

We, beneath its protection,
continue our stargazing this night.
Our lenses have already been set out.

Come then, all storms and clouds.
We long since gathered up our nerves.
Try as you might, we shall see.

ERIK VAN ACHTER

Emperor of the Hills and Valleys

Long live Gluteus Maximus, short-lived emperor of Rome,
he who drew a clear line between good and evil,
the Gluteal Line, a deep, visible crevasse
that divides all villains from heroes.

So little is known of you, successor to Aurelius,
eldest brother to the runt Gluteus Minimus.
How true is the revisionist history, I wonder,
that whispers of a Gluteus Medius between you?

We do recount, in hushed whispers, your nephew,
bestowed with an odd pear-shaped head,
clever Piriformus, owner of the small island
where once the Trojans had held firm.

Ah, to boldly remember when soldiers stood
cheek to cheek, ready to defend each street
from shallowest cracks to deepest trenches
against the tyranny of your enemies.

WILLIAM'S ANATOMY

Of course jokes were told, as always,
of how your brothers only ever would protect the rear,
ever behind your legions of men,
ever the butt of their jokes by the fires.

But no doubts were in their eyes, I'm sure,
when you straightened up the sore island
Coccyx single-handedly, betwixt old currents
near the great, gaping hole of Charybdis.

Truly, let no Roman man doubt fat old Gluteus,
as round and red as the apples he grew up on.
Had you only lived longer, by just a hair,
perhaps your lines never would have been crossed.

Every time a free woman's bottom bounces
in the night clubs of modern Rome,
let me raise a toast, a toast I say,
to the finest emperor this world has known.

ERIK VAN ACHTER

My Pear

My kingdom for a large pear.
Let its tantalizing taste
cleanse me of the bile of stress.
A pear does go so well with liver.
Its as if all the poisons of the day
just fade away into the mist.

Watch the pear juice leak
as I carefully open it,
forming ducts and rivers
amidst the landscape of the plate,
draining into that delectable liver.

My fork, be still,
I beg of you!
I know we have not said grace.
My bladder has the gall
to voice its concerns
as I fill myself with wine.

WILLIAM'S ANATOMY

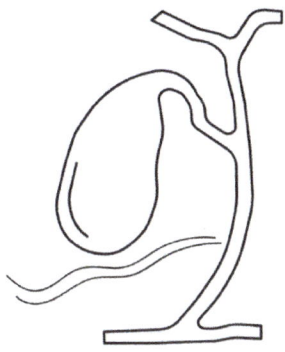

Worry not, my silly organs,
for I've both a liver and a pear
with which to easily cure myself
of any odd afflictions
that a quick drink might bring.

ERIK VAN ACHTER

The First Nerve

First of the cranial nerves,
like a short and stout river,
never to meet the ocean of the brainstem,
choosing instead to flow like a burst dam
through the cribriform plate.

But this river, this tiny river,
she carries with her such beautiful things.
The smell of azaleas in the courtyard.
A fresh scent of honey at breakfast
as it sinks into my toast.
A melody of odours arising
from the vast expanse of the woods.

Breathe nature into me,
oh noble first nerve.
Shout it through my cribriform.
Let my bulbs swell with the seasons,
cradling my rooster's comb,
my crista galli. Breathe it all in.

WILLIAM'S ANATOMY

Like the gods amidst ambrosia,
I smell the sea breeze,
my eyes rolling back with pleasure
as a short nerve fills itself to bursting.

Hold tight, tiny cribriform switchboard.
Lest my feeble thalamus explode,
unable to wield it all,
like a child holding an axe,
trying in vain to cleave in twain
this flow of information.

This stout river of data flows,
stoic in its duty but beautiful in execution.
Bless me with stimulation, I beg of you.
Let my cribriform tingle with the strain.

ERIK VAN ACHTER

Some lovers try positions that they can't handle.

Sandra was a lover of old wooden boats,
creaking and cracking like a skeletal band.
Leah was loony with her love for the moon,
a lady I never could quite understand.

Taylor lived in a room with three corners
when she wasn't asleep in her van.
Patricia could sleep on a pea and complain,
with the daintiest skin ever seen on land.

Tina was an irregular lass I might still love
had her sister not buried her head in the sand.
Tiffany always was the jealous type though,
so the surprise when I heard wasn't that grand.

Cathy, oh Cathy, the head of the pack
decided the guest list, from VIP to banned.
Hazel, with her hooked nose, never made the cut,
though I confess I was always her biggest fan.

WILLIAM'S ANATOMY

All of these ladies I loved in a year,
knew them as well as the back of my hand,
but none of these ladies ever loved me
and none of our dates ever went as planned.

Some lovers try positions that they can't handle.
It may not work out the way you expect
but I'm glad I tried them each, nonetheless.
It taught me a great deal about respect.

Sing me sweet symphonies of ladies in white,
ready to party and dressed for the night,
wearing pearls as pale and pretty as bone.
May some little lady come with me home.

ERIK VAN ACHTER

For more information and extra poems -

Visit | **www.erik.vanachter.com**

www.ingramcontent.com/pod-product-compliance
Lightning Source LLC
LaVergne TN
LVHW020419070526
838199LV00055B/3662